STONE GIRL

First published in 2019 by
The Dedalus Press
13 Moyclare Road
Baldoyle
Dublin D13 K1C2
Ireland

www.**dedaluspress**.com

ISBN 978-1-910251-48-5

Dedalus Press titles are available in Ireland
from Argosy Books (argosybooks.ie) and in the UK
from Inpress Books (www.inpressbooks.co.uk)

Cover image: 'Self Portrait with Camellia Branch', 1906/07
Artist: Paula Modersohn-Becker, 1876–1907
Technique: oil on wood. Location: Essen, Museum Folkwang
Photo: © Museum Folkwang Essen – ARTOTHEK

The Dedalus Press receives financial assistance from
The Arts Council / An Chomhairle Ealaíon.

STONE GIRL

MARY NOONAN

DEDALUS PRESS

ACKNOWLEDGEMENTS

Thanks to the editors of the following publications, in which some of these poems, or versions of them, have previously appeared: *Agenda, And Other Poems, Blackbox Manifold, The Compass, Cyphers, The Enchanting Verses, Ink, Sweat and Tears, Malpaís Review, The Manchester Review, New Hibernia Review, New Walk, One, PN Review, Poetry International, Poetry Ireland Review, Poetry London, Poetry Review, Southword, The Spectator, The High Window, The Irish Times, The Irish Examiner, The North, The Same, The Stinging Fly* and *The Well Review.* Thanks too to the editors of the following anthologies: *The Elysian* (New Binary Press, 2017) and *The Deep Heart's Core* (Dedalus Press, 2017).

Sincere thanks to Pat Boran at Dedalus Press for publishing this collection, and for his careful editing of the manuscript.

Heartfelt thanks to Hans Van Eijk, who published five of these poems in a limited edition under the title *Father* (Bonnefant Press, 2015), and the long poem *Flânerie of the Beaver* (Bonnefant Press, 2017).

I'm grateful to the Tyrone Guthrie Centre at Annahgmakerrig, where I spent time in 2014 and 2016, and where some of these poems were written.

Thanks to the Arts Council of Ireland for their generous granting of a Literature Bursary in 2014.

CONTENTS

⬅︎

NOTES / 86

                                Is that
a face at the skylight
in the grey slates? Whose?
Where is my sister?
The wire vibrates in the wind,
The sky spells rain,
The distant thunder of a plane
Pulls me up. Ah, doodle doo
                    Doodle doo.

—Matthew Sweeney, 'Doodle Doo'

Remember only that I was innocent
and that, like you today, mortal on this earth,
I had a face marked by the lines of laughter,
the crevices of pain – the face of a man or a woman.

        — Benjamin Fondane, 'L'Exode'
          (version, Mary Noonan)

for Matthew

The Moths

The artist is sitting, perfectly still,
by his mulberry tree, watching
it. He has been in that pose all day.

The white moths have flown
through my open window,
drawn by the light of a bedside lamp.

They are everywhere – cloaking
the walls, sleeping in the folds of sheets,
crawling over the shoes on the floor.

I try to flatten some with newspaper
but they are too many, and I lie down
among them. Soon, they cover me,

their anaemic plumes lining the creases
of my eyelids, lashes thrumming
to the sound of a thousand tiny wings

flicking. In the bed, I rustle. Moths are
spinning from hairs, slinking over the skin
of my scalp and pubis. I lie in a rictus.

In the morning, I walk on a flittered
bridal veil of wings, from bed to bathroom.
I pass the artist. He is sitting

by the fish tank, watching his black
piranha slip through cool water,
behind glass. Has he been there all night?

Equinox

I climb from under the man-hole,
the rat's nest of winter, find myself
on the beach at Kilkee, its perfect
horse-shoe bay. It must have been
beautiful once, before the crescent
bloomed its corona of bungalows.
Mid-March, I'm standing on the roof
of the year, looking down its long drag,
its high waves pulling and shoving,
arrogant prancers making like it's
in their gift to jerk the moon along
behind them, a ball of rags on a string,
make it go full circle, again and again.
Sky, powder-blue. Bladder wrack.
A sign on the bus shelter reads: 'Leave
nothing but your footprints'. Lines
of grey trees bend their bare backs
before the Atlantic winds, scraps
of black plastic cling, like tattered
shrouds, to the thorn. On the beach,
the equinoctial carnival is gearing up,
mustering to start again. Ah, start again.

The Bee Salon

They bring me the bees in ethanol.
Some have hung in their yellowing jars
for a hundred years, like these,
netted in the streets of Cagliari by a German
entomologist in the summer of 1909.

I tweezer Number 1 from her boozy amnion,
she's a shrivelled raisin and I must restore her
to beedom. The first step is to wash her
in my bee shampoo, a secret formula.
I pop the old lady in a bottle, give it a good shake –

oops! A leg has broken off … Never mind.
It can be glued back. I pluck the wrinkled worker
from the suds, lay her on a small cube of foam,
pierce her chest with a tiny pin, through
the wing-bud.

Drying is tricky. A hairdryer is hard on extremities,
but a small electric air-pump does the job.
The ancient wing-panes flap in the breeze,
and black and yellow stripes bloom in hoops
around the fuzzy torso.

Now it's time for the real work of the bee salon.
I lay her under the microscope and with my
small sable paintbrush I tease out her branched hairs,
matted and frizzy after her century-long sleep.
Her coiffure restored, I take up the tweezers again,

uncurl her eyelash-thin aerials: her antenna, her elegant
crop, her segmented legs, and yes, her knees.

That's Number 1 prinked and primped! She'll do.
I lay her in the shallow drawer, where she'll be joined
by her sisters. I only manage twenty a day.

My job title is 'preparator', they chose me for my fine
motor skills, and my eye for detail. I used to be
an organist. I often wonder about these tiny workers –
Number 1, for example: was she a builder of hexagonal
cells, who put her glands to service in the making of wax?

Or a mortuary bee, who ferried the colony's dead far
from the place of furious secretion, packing, sealing?

Flânerie of the Beaver

for Eugène Savitzkaya and Benjamin Fondane

The poet walks the city brandishing the breast-
bone of a magpie, his wish-bone, mark
of his poverty. He follows the ancient runnels
of the Bièvre, a river forced under the cobbles
of the Latin Quarter centuries ago.

He is tracing the tracks of the beavers
who once gnawed the bark of chestnut trees
on the river bank. He wants to be a beaver,
to shake off his man's carcass. As he walks,
he meditates on his foot, how crucial it is

to his survival, and dreams of growing his coccyx
into a tail, or releasing precious castoreum
from the glands in the castor sac behind his
testicles. If he has money, he stops for red wine
on rue Mouffetard, at 'The Glass With One Foot'.

Beavers use their musky secretion to scent their terrain.
This is his territory now, and he sniffs as he walks
the lanes to the bench behind St Médard, stretches
his ears to listen to the creaking of the tombs in
the old cemetery. What he hears is the howling

of the convulsing women who contorted their bodies
here in the seventeeth century, working themselves
into states of mystical ecstasy at the grave of
the ascetic François de Pâris. Their moans
tickle his ears, as they offer their pear-fig-melon-

shaped breasts to the young Jansenist priests.
Their resting place later passed into the hands of
a locksmith, who sold the collar-bones
of the convulsionists as treasure. The poet
sits and listens to the chorus of crying tombs,

wailing women and neighbourhood cats, then
walks on to the Arena of Lutèce, the Roman
gladiatorial circus of Paris. In the circle of blood,
now covered in sand, he chooses his spot, where
he places two blocks of wood, dons his hessian pants,

a woolen cap and his reading glasses, then flips
his body upside-down, his head between the two
blocks, his legs perpendicular in the air.
In this posture, he reads aloud from a lengthy work.
His gentle voice booms round the amphitheatre,

and pages, once read, are thrown to the wind.
Having vomited his verse, he flops to the sand
and lies there for some time, muttering 'Et je ne
suis pas fatigué, et je ne suis pas fatigué', before
gathering the pages with the help of circling children.

He walks on further, to the river, the site of the old
Gobelins tapestry workshops. He fancies he can
smell the foul effluent from the tanneries that
once lined the riverbank. The poet locates
his favourite chestnut tree, sits there

dreaming of the long incisors he will grow,
of how he will learn to bite off his testicles
when threatned by hunters, fling them in their
faces, and of how he will preen his lustrous pelt
in the sun. He wonders if he will have any memory

of the man he was: that he was innocent, that he
had tried to craft strong paper boats, float them
on the Bièvre, that he had ended carrying
the breastbone of a magpie around Paris, and that
like you today, mortal on this earth, he had a face

marked by the lines of laughter, the crevices
of pain, the face of a man or a woman, who now
has the face of a beaver, a reed between its teeth.

Self-Portrait with Camellia Branch

homage to Paula Modersohn-Becker

Your painting of a girl in a blue worsted dress
blowing a flute in a birch forest – a cage
with knotted silver bars – could be a beginning,

a way to tell why you ran from Teufelsmoor
to Paris, where crowds were fêting a tower
on the Seine, experimenting with light.

Four times in seven years you ran to the life-
drawing classes, where they let you sketch
the nudes. You knew what you could learn from

the mummy portraits in the Louvre, those eyes
without pupils, facing into the after-life.
In Rodin's studio, you saw it was possible to draw

and not care what people thought and you
were able to let go at last, dive into the whirring
life of skin and amber and camellia branches

held aloft in the hands of melancholy children.
How you rushed to get it all out, writing Otto that you
would never go back to him, never have his child,

asking your sister to photograph you naked so that
you could paint your nude 'Self-Portrait on the Sixth
Wedding Anniversary', your belly round,

a string of yellow beads between your breasts –
Schade! – the word that flew from your throat
as you died, aged thirty-one, days after the birth.

Ah Schade, Paula ! What a shame it was!
You began by painting very old women, their hands
crossed in their laps, and you finished with your portraits
of girls, pressing red and yellow flowers to their hearts.

Clotho

homage to Camille Claudel

People expected the beautiful Clotho,
youngest of the Fates, with her spindle
and her insouciance, spinning the thread
of life, deciding who would be born, who
would die. But in your plaster, she was
a naked crone, skin sagging from breasts
and belly, small head yanked back by
the ragged tresses that sprawled from
her scalp to the mud at her feet.
A raised hand tore at the baffling mane.

Your second Clotho was in marble.
She was destined for the Luxembourg
Museum, but the gallery wouldn't have her,
fearing people's response to the dereliction
flaunted by the toothless hag. Where did she
end up? She passed through many hands,
including Rodin's, before disappearing.
Then you pulled off your own vanishing act –
No ! Other hands – a mother's, a brother's –
signed you away to the asylum where

you would spend the next thirty years
trying to forget your Clotho.
Was it Rodin's shunning, or the squalor
of your room on the Quai de Bourbon
that turned you into the self-cutting, cat-
whispering witch who scoured the river's
banks at night, collecting clay? Maybe.
But when they caught you and taught you
to revile your art, you grew into the scandal
you had chiselled: an old woman, deciding nothing.

Rue St Paul

I see them standing in the small room, the one I rented
for them on rue St Paul – *Hôtel du Septième Art.*
A couple from Ireland, in their fifties, in a hotel

on a street crammed with shabby-chic antique shops.
Do they look out of place? They had lived in London,
and in a provincial city, but their blood

was of the rural parishes of county Cork.
I'm older now than they were then.
In their unfashionable clothes and poor hair-cuts

they stand by the bed and marvel at the framed
black-and-white posters on the walls – Bogie, Bacall,
James Dean – as I outline my plans to shuttle them

between the Sacré Coeur and the Eiffel Tower, taking in
a *bateau-mouche* trip on the Seine, and they give
themselves up, willingly, to my banal tourism.

But my mother, menopausal, got up each morning at dawn
to walk the *quartier* in search of its wild cats. Maybe she met
the ghosts of the animals from the zoo put there by a king.

And my father scrutinised the French racing pages,
trying to figure out the PMU betting system. He might
have got on well with the Portuguese migrants

who lived on the street in the fifties, when TB was rampant.
I stand there looking up at the boarded windows
of the cheap hotel, its fake Hollywood nostalgia

so at odds with the street's seventeenth-century houses
where the spectres of monks and merchants shuffle
between the roof beams. I see my parents

standing by the bed in the small room, desperate to
show me they understood what all the fuss was about.
I hope I was kind to them, but I doubt it.

Racing Results

i.m. my father

A knot of men clusters under the town clock –
five past seven on a hot July evening.
Stragglers make their way, jocular salutes
chiming with the chorus of slagging, the lighting
of Woodbines, Sweet Afton.

Men with a purpose, many without a job,
putting off the day when they will board
the Rosslare train. They have their rituals,
their places: the football pitch, the snooker hall,
the handball alley. And here, nightly.

You are in their number, twenty years old, thin
and very brown from all your running and cycling
in the sun, shoe-laces secured by tight knots
tied three times.

At 7.10, the Cork bus comes into view,
pulls up at Welch's the Hardware.
The driver greets a waiting boy, throws a bundle
bound with twine onto the footpath.
The late edition of the *Evening Echo*.

He carries his parcel carefully,
men ambling behind him in procession
to the paper shop. Outside again, they stand
stock-still, scouring the back pages –
will luck be a lady tonight?

A few shillings the richer or poorer
in a town with no telephones, no radios,
where the evening bus brings the late edition,
news of Sandown, Chepstow, Goodwood.

In God's House

The folk-group, mid-nave, touchy-feely, is harbouring
a crow, cawing off-key and someone is hacking at
guitar-strings while my father sings along to hymns
he does not know, '70s hits from the Singing Nun –
Oh Lord, let me be your sanctuareee –

practising his technique of almost chiming, just a beat
out of step. The missionary priest, on tour from Armagh,
is telling us, very slowly, about the Real Presence –
he really is there! – his Northern consonants eerily
softened, the better to permeate us with the glories

of the tabernacle. He raises the host and keeps it up there,
whispering to himself – or to Him – secrets
we are denied, then pours wine and holds a silver chalice,
lingeringly, to his lips as my father removes his glasses
again, rubbing the red orbits of his eyes, over and over,

making loud breathing sounds, like a man who has climbed
Kilimanjaro and is working his diaphragm on the summit,
taking in huge bowls of air, filling his lungs with
snow-capped peaks and Tanzanian sky, in and
out and in and out, or like a boy among rows of boys

doing chest expansion drill in a Hitler youth camp,
in and out and in and out until the man next to him sneezes
and he tut-tuts loudly, following up with a prayer that
ricochets through several rows – 'Jesus!' – and no, he will not
take his stick as he hobbles the long walk to the host.

Into the Night

You fling yourself out the door into the wind
and start to row yourself down the steep hill
with your standard issue steel stick, working it
along the dark path, clickety-click, clickety-click.
It's a path you would know with your eyes closed,
the old Richmond Hill you cycled up and down
as a boy, in all weathers, coming and going from
the house perched on top. You shuttle along at first,
taking full advantage of your exit velocity, clickety-
click, clickety- flop against the rail, breathe heavily,
rattle on. At the bottom, you tilt into Patrick Street
and fluorescent lighting, poke at the white rounds
winking on the ground, checking for coins, finding
gum. You have forgotten
your glasses, and so your vision is that of a small
subterranean animal, tunnelling with its fore-paws.
Staggering now, you keel against walls, your flittered
left hip giving way. A passer-by gives you a second
glance, wonders. Your cap is pulled tightly over
the bald eyebrows you shave off every other day,
along with cheek bristle. You propel yourself on,
slashing the wind, and the dark. You don't know
where you are going, or why.

In the House

I am back in the house, with my father reading
the same paragraph of newsprint, over and over,
as the light fades and the letters break up and slide
over the page and he tries to corral them, dogged
in his conviction that if he keeps herding them,
they will stay there, on the page, in the house where
a trail of tissue-marbles leads to the bathroom, with
its tiny squares of paper, folded over and over, then
laid out in neat rows along the window-ledge. Is it
too late for me to write my prayer on them, open
the window and release the wind horses to the air?

Paper is sacred in this house where every shred
becomes a miniature envelope for elfin letters
posted and collected by an origami master who
spends hours swaying on his wasted hip as day
morphs into night and he sweeps the drift of snow
from the black tiles, or picks each white fleck from
the ribs of his cords. I wish I'd said goodbye
to the man whose step I waited to hear, bounding
up the stairs, whose cool hand I loved to feel
on my forehead, whose 'How's the patient today?'
made my heart jump. I wish I'd said goodbye,
before the ancient shape-shifter came to build
his nests of lint, his hillocks of gristle.

Vanishing Act

We can no longer say goodbye,
no more take our leave of each
other. Now, I must slip in and
out of the compartments of your
world, where the dead move freely
in the antechambers, where to go
through a door is to be erased
forever and long-dead fathers
are always just a staircase away.
I will pace now in the *salle des pas
perdus*, losing my way, entering
by one door, exiting by another,
appearing before you courtesy of
a complex of sliding panels and
vanishing again without saying
the farewell word, vaporising
into the great waiting hall where
all doors lead. What do you make
of these random comings and goings,
your visitors always arriving without
announcement or appointment,
and leaving by the same slippery
method? How does it feel to be
the still centre of these revolving
portals, you, the empty waiting-room
where only ghosts stop, on their way
to Heaven knows where?

Body

We never touched, all the years
of our long story, kept our distance.
Your cheekbone – chiseled, bristly –
was a strange land. Even the word *body*
was banned – it never left your mouth.
But now I'm all over you, an octopus
popping pills on your tongue at breakfast,
allowing your false teeth to plop
into my palm at night. I lather soap
on your salt-and-pepper skin, draw
the blade slowly over your jaw, waver
round the small apple. I undress you,
open the shower door, prod you in.
I beg you to send your hand back out,
squeeze shampoo on your palm,
tell you to rub it well into your scalp.
You shiver, cringe, tell me my hands
are icy cold. I never thought I'd see
my father's penis. And after the long haul
of hours spent cajoling you to lie down
under the covers, you grab my hand,
lock it in yours, won't let it go.

River, Man

for Liz

The great river is watering the dark,
irrigating the central plain with black floods.
The callows are brimming, no channel
or lock can stem the seepage.
Long November nights caul the families
creeping from farms, bits of furniture
clamped under arm-pits. As the torrent
breaks the weirs at Parteen, you loll
your head on your breast bone, flower
broken on the stem, as if resting

on the shoulder of the farmer's daughter
from Park, Galbally, who gave birth to you
above the Bus Bar, Fermoy, in 1927.
You were a running boy from the off,
lining up neighbour kids for races round
the fields behind the hilltop house, until
you started to tog out for the foreign game –
so small, you could run between
the goalie's legs – and you ran, you ran
over all those water-logged pitches.

Afraid to lie down now, you spend your nights
crooking your spine in a chair, like a bent
clothes-hanger, so that the fluid in your
eye-sockets is sluicing forward to fill
the sacks of your upper and lower lids.
Water is pooling in your calves and ankles,
and your skin, under pressure, is breaking
down, letting the salt liquid seep through,
trickle in small rivulets down the shins
you guarded with pads on the soccer pitch.

The great river is in trouble. Its drainage
is failing and soon the swollen waters will
break the ramparts and you will be carried
away, past the Famine Relief Wall, past
the Young Men's, past the Bus Bar, up
Barrack Hill and beyond the garrison pitch
to Kilcrumper, where wet sods will slow
the running bones, clog ball and socket,
and you will lie down.

Goodnight, Vienna

I want them to take you, on arrival
and then nightly, to an airy room in
pastel shades, with polished mahogany
tables, gilt rococo mirrors and ormolu
ceilings – Café Einstein, the best
coffee-house in Vienna.

You never liked coffee, and that's not
why you're here. You've never been to
Vienna either, nor had your mother
before you. Hers was the best apple-tart
in Ireland, you said, made with rough,
sour apples, lashings of beet sugar
from the factory in Mallow, and Bird's
instant custard from the tin –

but Dad, this *apfelstrudel* is the angels'
food. Come in, take off your astrakhan
hat, dive into the stacked filaments of
fruit, layered with raisins and almonds,
rolled in pastry light as a snow-flake,
dusted with cinnamon and castor sugar
and set adrift in a warm pool of eggy
sauce speckled with tiny vanilla seeds.

I want you to go swimming, night after
night in that continental custard
(custard that's had manners put on it
at some Alpine finishing school) in a
room beyond time, where your *knock-out*,
as you call it, never happened, where
the tables are covered in white linen,

32

where the waiters smile and bow as you
lick your spoon, then lick it again.

Blues

Like the sapphire eyes of the African wood owl
I saw once in a zoo, yours glinted and darted
as you chased the ball down the oh-so-many
football fields. Your grand-daughter, who lives
near the Arabian desert, said they were 'the sea'.

I would have said cerulean: between sea and sky.
Or the cornflowers of harvest meadows.
Mottled now, rheumy. One of them blind,
the other held a cataract dammed behind
the nerve, worn down by decades of peering

at columns of digits pencilled in tall ledgers,
or following numbered horses as they sailed
over fences on the far side of the track.
At the graveyard, one Sunday, you pressed
your cheek against the stone, touched

the letters, asked me to call the names –
Daniel, Jane, Jack, Marie – Ah, Marie!
And then came the Sunday when you opened
your eyes and turned two black irises on me –
lampblack, sucking in the light; black

as plastic sacks flapping on hedges in February;
the black of paper eyes glued to a cheap toy.
All blue had drained out, condensed to air
the singing blue, the dancing blue, the blue
of flowers and stones. The blues of you.

Like an Orange

La terre est bleue comme une orange – Paul Éluard

It's hard to stay standing on this blue
ball as it spins. Its surface is covered
in pocked matter that wants to draw
you down, pull you in. The river's rim
is smashed by angry tides, and signs
warn that the water wants to suck me
into the holes that lie beneath.

You tried running on the spot when
you could no longer walk. I loved
your wild refusal, your challenge
to the earth's compulsion, you,
the blind jockey riding the bucking
bronco, hanging onto the scruff
of its neck as it jigged, pain

ricocheting through your broken
ball-and-socket joints. And when
at last you did fall off, I held my hand
to the nape of your neck, found
your heat still hiding there, among
the small hairs. The undertaker
wadded your upper lip, puffed

your cheeks with embalming fluid,
padded your rib-cage, so skinny.
A handsome corpse. But where
were you? 'Dying is hard,'
said the butcher's wife. 'They're afraid
to let go.' As if they were separate,
an alien species, nothing to do with

the creepers over the zesty surface
of the orange. I walk the river's bank,
a mummy, a zombie, a robot pre-
programmed to march on, till the road
runs out or a wave jumps up or
a branch breaks and I am flung from
the blue ball, as it spins, reckless.

Haiku for my Father

Crocuses open
Your bones lie perfectly still
In softening earth

Fractured

For your first, mortuarial
anniversary, I managed it,
my finest trick: I became you

yes, I pulled off the skin-
changing thing by flinging
myself up in the air and banging

back down on my left
arm: banjaxed. I was
a barmy, splintered Boney

in a black sling as they drove me
to your anniversary mass,
fuming at having to be zipped up

buckled in, shovelled out,
turning the air foul with my
locker-room bawling

raining hexes on all drivers,
threatening blue murder,
boxing the enemy with one arm tied

around my neck/your neck,
head-butting the sun, moon and
stars for their part in the conspiracy.

Morse on Skin

I've wondered through fifty-odd
years, why July brings such

gloom to me born in June
first-born of Irish parents

St Stephen's Hospital, Fulham
my father machine-minder

thin and sun- tanned, bounding
down the ward holding me high

saying She's got ten fingers and
toes, anyway ! Oh, happy happy

then back to the room in Clapham
my mother stre tched on the bed

crying, and me picked up for
feeding and cleaning. The silence

of the grave except for the sobbing
I learned to lie very still. July

the morse being etched on my skin,
tapping out an ending

Since, other months have scratched
their codes : eighteen

Aprils for my mother

one Feb   ruary, month of laying
my father   in the ground

The months   revolve, triggering
skin's memory   of other skins

the impossibility of their loss

Ferryman

I step onto the Shaky Bridge as night
is falling and sheets of rain are slapping
at my face, no let-up for three months now.
A hooded figure sways in the murk.
'You go ahead and pass me out, Ma'am',
he says. 'I've had a few drinks. I'm tired.'
I walk past, mulling over the 'Ma'am'
and the 'pass me out'. Was he about to
pass out? In passing him, was I wiping
him out? Was someone passing on?
In French, 'passeur' is the ferryman.
Was this him then, washed up by the storms
and walking slant across a dodgy bridge
in Cork, swigging from a cider bottle
and tired, so tired from hauling his cargo
of souls through the filthy fog mugging
the swollen waters of the Lee? I leap
like a goat off the bridge and onto slippery
steps spiralling upward. The glassy ground
is littered with broken white china.

Elysian

Through green, I view the city's remains. Green
glass of this colossal tower, relic of the Tiger years
whose sole lodger is me, riding the crystal warship
high above what used to be the skyline, now
the water line. Pea green from pole to pole.

I spy with my little eye three green copper cupolas,
the crowns of City Hall, St Francis and the Courthouse
floating on moss-green clouds. A golden flying fish,
the city's flag, is still intact. I crouch above algal infinity,
a hawk plotting the horizon in vectors.

But my vantage is not safe. Bodies float by. Debris
of green cranes. At first, the floor show was all
uprooted trees, and cars. Then came the stampede.
Murders, cullings. I helped to fling the dead from
the penthouse balconies. Now I lie alone on cool marble.

The emerald light of evening floods the empty rooms,
long redundant. I listen for sounds, whirring of a lift
in the shaft, the whoosh of automatic doors.
Ghost lift, ghost doors. When I sleep, I go back
to the old city –

the mysteries of the timber yard on Water Street,
where my father worked; the temptations of the sidings
of the West Cork Railway on Albert Quay; the olive
majolica tiles of the Eglinton Street Swimming Baths,
bobbing before chlorine-pricked eyes;

our flat on Lower Road, where water rats danced
over our beds as we slept. My sister and I would play
at skipping on the docks, watching for the timber boats
coming up the river from Sweden, the banana boats
gliding in from Africa, or Jamaica. And we would wait

for hours in the rain to snatch our prize: rotting bananas
flung to us by the black sailors. That was our playground,
the port where Dutch merchants built their watery empire,
a market where Bordeaux wine was swopped for butter.
I close my eyes, try to conjure butter,

the faces of my father and my sister. Fields of flowers.
Elysian fields, where the gods went to die.

Perch

The waiter has the precision of a surgeon
as he rotates the blade clockwise
in the small pillows of your face.
I, in turn, slice the char-grilled silk pocket,
a delicacy in Ribarsko Ostrvo, place it
in my mouth, snug with the flesh of my cheek.
We're waltzing cheek-to-cheek now, Perch,
I'm tasting the sludgy intimacy of your face,
a face you loved to nudge through the rippled
surface of the Danube while the Canada geese
honking overhead sent tremors all along
the listening canals of your body.

Sea-Drift

The high rollers are pouring jade
onto the shore, and sandpipers
are snoking in the shale, finding
bits of green plastic twine, shreds
of orange net, sea glass, a dry claw.
I ask the bay to tell me my name
but it stays stumm, making like it's
deaf as the posts holding up the fence,
deaf as the smooth rock-eggs laid
in the white clover. And I am dumb,
dumb as the grass skirts on the dunes,
doing the hoola-hoola to the wind's
tune, dumb as the council's path
breaking up beneath my feet like
rubble in a breaker's yard. Then
I stumble on a hidden track zig-
zagging along the dune-tops and
spongy loam massages my soles
as I sink prints in the marram,
marking a path for the next cast-
away to comb the sand, discover
the more forgiving way back.

The Invader

for Matthew

A walrus on dry land, you were
bulky and clumsy and implausibly
hairy, likely to bump into furniture,
send small, gilded things flying.
The kitchen shrank at the sight of
you, penning your shopping list on
a shred of paper, a lime leaf
trembling as it bares its veins
to the early summer sun.

Your lettering was such as the elves
might have made, when leaving notes
for the shoemaker. Your *salade de boeuf
à la parisienne* was a millefeuille of beef
slivered into veils – Scheherazade
must have worn them to mask her
face and body as she spun her tales,
keeping death on the other side of night.

Bright orange wings – Vanessa Atalanta,
scintilla astray in the Mojave desert –
were once tomatoes. Bread you shaved
to be thin as the collar-bone of a hare,
worn thin by the lapping of water,
or lace, woven in a *beguinage*, from
threads almost invisible.

Now I see you. Not a walrus, but
an oyster, puzzled to find yourself
growing flesh round a grain of sand,

burrowing into holes in the sea to let
waves roll, and roll over you, score
the music of the world's waters
on the opaline droplet stowed
in your mantle.

Travelling Light

You're standing behind plate glass
in your kimono, looking out on that lake
in northern Michigan, hoping to catch sight
of the black squirrels or the black bears
or the ghosts of the Chippewa Indians.

I'm here walking the Grand Canal, where
the ghost of Kavanagh hangs around his
bronze cast. I snap him with my iPhone.
snap the beech trees, turning rusty,
the mallards washing in leaves.

Send. Send. The poet wrote that the green
waters of the canal were pouring him
redemption. I want the phone to beam
the leafy-with-love banks to the shores
of Mullett Lake as a cold wind blows in

and you stand there in your Japanese robe
day-dreaming of flying fish and flowers
bending and bowing in underwater
caves, and a man running all the way
to the moon, his light shell-house
bobbing on his back.

Gare du Nord

We sit, looking across at the façade.
When I'm gone, you say, remember
me here. I think about that, imagine
myself alone at this street-side café,
the massive stone of the station filling
my eyes, the marble goddesses, each
named for a northern city – Arras, Lille,
Rouen – louring down at me.

We know it well, know each corbel,
key- and corner-stone, as if by heart.
You are consumed, as always, by the
wild parade of the living, the aubergine
women, armed with batons and walkie-
talkies, stalking the parked cars,
the skate-boarding transvestites yakking
on mobiles, the louche boys patrolling
the tables, on the look-out for gormless
tourists. The ragged, the maimed,
the pigeons.

Thinking of all that, and of the sand
swirling round our toes in the
Tuileries, of the sweet (caramel,
biscuit) and salty (stale piss) smells
of summer metros, I conclude that
if I were ever to glide up, without you,
from the underworld of northern trains
into the dazzling light of a hot, dusty Paris,
order a rosé at the Terminus Nord
and look across at the railway basilica –

the hellish white of the portal would
tear the sight from my eyes, the bald-eyed
furies balancing on their pedestals would
swoop and strike me with axe, sword
and knife, passing boys would rob me
and I would stumble away to wander
the streets of Paris as once I wandered
alone among peacocks in a paradisical
New Delhi garden, seeing nothing.

Do you really think I could look again
at these end-of-the-line pillars and porticoes,
these blind granite women, remembering you,
and not myself be turned to stone?

Still Life with Pigeons

I

The nude statues on rue du Faubourg St Denis – she holding a full-blown globe, he a crescent moon – had a ball of blood-smeared feathers at their feet when I snapped them with my iPhone. And a couple of feral pigeons lay on their backs behind a plate glass shop-front on rue de Belleville as I walked by, bird sinew mixed with the dust of cinder-blocks, toppled pillars. How did they come to be inside for the swing of the wrecking-ball, the thump of the sledgehammer, doomed to lie framed, side-by-side, under plaster-of-Paris snow?

II

Pigeons are dying in this city. My apartment looks onto a gable-end that does not show French windows with pelmets of wrought-iron *fleur-de-lys*. Instead, biscuit-cutter apertures puncture concrete, like judas spy-holes. I watch the pigeons fidget on the ledges, the building become columbarium, with nest-holes for the breeding and fattening of squabs. But this is no rubblestone dovecote, hub of hectic production for the tables of abbots and barons. The block is more reliquarium, mausoleum for the housing of ashes.

III

The bird deaths are getting to me. Last night you flambéed chicken breasts in cognac, added red wine, silky shallots and button mushrooms. We stripped the *coq au vin* of its chocolate-brown robes, and later your lips moved over my limbs, prolonging the fleshy feast. But I'm not a collared – or a turtle – dove! Not a chicken, in the spring of its short life, nor a lone swallow flying back to Capestrano! I'm too young to have my small neck ruffed by a pigeonhole or my bones picked clean ; too young to be pulverised for the cinerary jars of the columbarium ; too young to lie frozen beside my mate, behind glass.

Caryatids

The stone women of Paris are draped
in folds of lapidary gauze, baring breasts
and bellies as they hang out under cupolas
or balance entablatures on their heads,
as they might have balanced baskets when
dancing in the walnut groves of home.

Their faces are cinereal, all colour long
drained out. No one will ever invite them
for a drink, tell them to loosen up.
Calcified now for all time, they are in control
of this one task, unassailable in the curvature
of their stout arms and thighs. Touch me not.

And if someone calls out obscenities, these
bounce off their ears like sleet, or the feathers
of pigeons. Their smiles are fixed, and their
hearts – well, if they have hearts, they must be
small and hard as the shell of a walnut.
I drift in the city of stone, looking only upward

until I reach the Hôtel Biron, and Rodin's
Fallen Caryatid Carrying Her Stone. Here
is the banished angel reduced to human scale:
a girl. Crouching on the artist's plinth,
her lowered head rests on her right arm, while
both hands bend to her left shoulder where

a great block sits. How did she come to be
squirming here, at the eye-level of tourists?
Was it a bomb that toppled her from her perch,
forced her to descend to where she must carry

the very rock from which she will be cut –
a girl hefting the womb that will birth her,
press her to the dirt?

Ascenseur

On the other side of this wall
an old woman is rattling hangers
in a mahogany wardrobe and
pulling open wooden drawers.
I imagine her widowed, small-
boned, arranging bibelots,
a lifetime of strung beads.
When asked, she will say there was
shouting. There was shouting and
banging of doors, and long silences.
One day, a man sobbed on the balcony.

On the other side of this door,
an antique cage rises and falls
through a shaft of seven floors
cut deep into marble and curling
bronze. A missile-shaped weight
creeps up and down the outer wall,
hauling the iron box on its pulleys,
jolting it into motion, sometimes
stopping halfway between floors.
From the bed, I listen to the clank
of the old machine, the slap of grill doors.

The Resonator

I can hear the drops falling from the small faces
trapped in the masonry of Paris: caryatids, satyrs,
lions – all are weeping. My fugue is at an end,
I must leave my niche in the Ninth where I have
stood still, a small stone general in a nook
emerging only to prowl my square mile round
rues Charon, Milton, Hippolyte Lebas with
the bad-boy ghosts from Le Chat Noir

on the street of the martyrs. My bedroom
is an echo chamber, thrumming with notes of
bells and rain, and at its centre – me, the resonator
for a daily symphony: the flying feet of a small child,
glissando across the upstairs parquet, arpeggios
of creaks made by flat and heeled shoes,
the syncopated clanking of pipes, counterpoint
of whirring, the lift in its shaft.

The study is a bath of sounds where, overhead,
parents wash their child and their dishes
in the same bowl, and I am in that bowl too,
being splashed or sluiced. Each morning at eight,
the boy drops a glass marble on the boards above
and the heavy bead bounces three times –
reverberations of a crystal cat's eye in the silence
of the morning room, mind just opening to the day.

Professor McCracken's Lecture on Skin

The American medievalist delivered her talk
on the power of fur in the Middle Ages.
The higher the rank, the more ostentatious

the garments of hide. Kings wore full sable
houppelandes to show their dominion
over all the creeping creatures, the right to take life

and wear the skin of the vanquished as trophy.
While she summoned French lords draped
in the prestige of marten and weasel, I couldn't help

noticing her name, wondering if she knew that
'craiceann' is the Gaelic for skin. She showed
slides of the covering of the private parts

in twelfth-century images of Adam and Eve
leaving Paradise, and mused on the mobility
of skin – its ability to conceal and disclose –

but what came to my mind were Irish and Scottish
tribes herding goats on hillsides, skinning them
to make panniers for humping turf from the bog,

discovering that weathered hide, when hit with fist,
made a hollow drumming; calves rounded up
in a haggard, yielding their flesh to burning oak,

their skin to the monks, who dried and scraped it
to make vellum for the missals they inscribed with
gold-leaf and cochineal; groups of men slipping

from small coves into northern seas in coracles
made from hide stretched over curved lathes –
skin boats they called 'naomhógs', little holy ones.

Sylvia's Books

I've taken your little books with me,
the blue and the red, Sylvia's books,
thin, clothbound, you carried them
in your pockets in the '70s, memorising
every word and line-break, all the
cutting little poppies, little hell flames,
and lizards airing their tongues
in the crevice of an extremely small shadow.
Their spines are cracked, their lettering
gilded splinters, and I have flung them
in a sack of indifferent books, so that
they emerge frazzled, out of breath.

I should take much more care of them,
these two old Sylvias who have brazened it out
down the long years. They should be sitting
in bath-chairs on the sea-front at Worthing,
knees snug in moss-and-heather mohair,
papery eyelids closing in soft afternoon sunshine.
I should be wearing Bruges lace gloves when
I hold them, these books that tell me of you
in your twenties, learning to do battle as a poet,
loving Sylvia, her little pilgrim scalp axed
by Indians, her million soldiers running,
redcoats every one.

With Thee I Swing

Above me
the silver birch with my initials stretched
upward to its far-off father, the moon.
— Matthew Sweeney, 'The Blue Hammock'

You've torn your hands in three unlikely places
while lifting our cases from a rack, shredding
skin on both forefingers, scoring a deeper wound
at the root of a thumb. We're making our way
to Berlin, to bury John.

At Marienfeld his urn is placed in a wall,
Billy Holiday's 'With Thee I Swing' inscribed
in gold on a plaque. Lupins are blooming,
your hands bleeding through sticking-plaster
as we walk down leafy Jenbacherweg, the frontier

between east and west where you spent days
together, years, writing, writing – the poet's
handbook, then the thriller that skewered
the dirty heart of poetry – building, line upon line,
sometimes shouting, furiously, but always

ending with John banging out some old jump-jive tune
on the piano and joining you to drink white Burgundy
on the canopied terrace. You tell me you've lost
your other half, and though I'm your girlfriend
of seven years, I know that the comrade who ran

with you across the wild Germanic borderlands,
the blood-brother who pledged his word,
has gone, leaving you alone here. With me.

Letter to Cal

from the correspondence of Elizabeth Bishop

Well, I suppose no one's heart is good
for much till it's been smashed to bits.
But no more doctors, I'm going to get
my repair work done at the doll hospital
from now on. I'm exhausted all over, but
particularly the face, which must come from

wearing a horrible fixed grin for so long.
I've put some Arden lotion in the ice-box
and am looking forward to lying down and
putting a nice cold washcloth full of it on
my poor hypocritical features. I wish
you'd come. We could go bone-fishing.

They're the greatest fish there is – very small.
You have to pole through the mangrove keys
silently. And in June, there's tarpon –
that's moonlight night-fishing. Ravishing
but hard to catch. The Polish girl and a boy
from the hotel are teaching me pool,

such a useful thing to know. And Sunday
I'm going to the cockfights. But I do wish
someone would ask me to go to the races –
I'm dying to. Thank you so much for the
'Glass Eye and Supplies'. Only you know
how fond I am of glass eyes.

I used to have relatives with glass eyes when
I was small, and for some reason I worried

because I thought they wouldn't go to Heaven.
I don't think I was ever fully reassured.
When you write my epitaph, you must say
I was the loneliest person who ever lived.

October Jazz

The crows are lining up on the scalloped roof
of the old church – a long row of monks
gossiping, squabbling. It's the hour when the dog
goes home, and the wolf comes out, the hour the clocks
shuttled backward last night.

Almost Samhain, the time of burials and unearthings,
and the city is teeming with jazz musicians.
But here, on this hill, I'm like a sole survivor,
swimming slowly through the thick silence
that hangs in the air after the dust has settled.

As I pass the church, I turn and see myself,
in the silence, twenty years earlier,
in my new duck-egg-blue silk shirt and
my black high-heeled suede boots, all set
to storm the jazzy town, hopped-up

on the adrenalin of time spent spritzing
the house, putting fresh sheets on the bed,
fresh-cut flowers in the bowl, ready for
the man I'll meet at the concert, prepared
to be surprised by the dancer who will find me

among the sweating bodies squeezing to the bar.
I'm the bystander, the one wanting to run
from the crepe soles squelching in beer-soaked pile.
And I do. Out of the silence I come, clambering back
up the hill, past the church, past midnight.

No crows, but a radiant moon, a midnight-blue sky,
stars playing ten pin bowling and riffing on Mingus's

'Wednesday Night Prayer Meeting', brass hounds
growling round my brain. The first frost is stinging
my earlobes, hairs are standing up along my legs.

Clambering back, the decades-lighter-me
vaporizes into the twilight, and I give the friary of crows
a last look, walk on.

Apollonian

So here you are, in Palma de Mallorca, in *Bunker's*,
the cool bistrot named for the god-like surfer
who bailed in Malibu at the age of twenty-eight,
couldn't ride the wave of his father's sugar millions.

But that troubled son is nothing to both of you,
sitting opposite your teenagers – a girl and a boy,
olive-skinned, strong-boned. Are you on holiday?
You stare, wide-eyed, and smile while they

do all the talking, their dark brows moving
in waves of knowledge and humour. Delicate
and tough, they look made for the new world –
already, they know more than you, though

they don't know what a tightrope act it was
to deliver them and their mother-of-pearl spines –
once fragile as spun sugar, or linnets' throats –
to this table. And they don't know if they in turn

will have to hoist your old bones on their backs
and hike across a mountain pass to safety, or
how far they will have to travel on without you.
What's it like to be looking into the radiant disks

of these Apollonian faces, reflecting you and
your parents and glimmers of the ancestors
who survived, the man who had to let go
of a small boy's hand, watch him slip into the deep

as he tried to swim against the eddying vortex,
or the woman who, starving, followed a procession
of ants and raided their store of grain in order to
feed her family? All of that, pressing for a hearing

beneath the silken skin of these, your flawless children.

Kensington High Street

i.m. my mother

I exit the rush-hour underground and it's you
I find, hurrying along the night-time street.
You came over in '56, you and my father seeking
work, too poor to marry in Fermoy. You found
your first London job in the basement of Barkers.

I scrutinise the old chocolate-brown building,
no longer a genteel department store, the lower floor
a giant Whole Foods mall. But you're here, you're
here in the geometric Art-Deco façade – was it built
in 1930, the year of your birth? They've put you

in Haberdashery, buffing the walnut counter till your face
is ablaze in amber. But when you get the chance
you pull open a shallow drawer, lift a spool of ribbon –
'eau de nil' – feel the watered silk between your fingers
as you measure it against the brass yard-stick.

I cross the road to St Mary Abbots, its gothic shadows
skipping round floodlit gargoyles and buttresses.
What do you make of the steel-grey steeple? Shoppers
swirl about the fulcrum of its pencil-thin elegance,
oblivious to the ease with which it spikes the Kensington sky.

You cross the road in your lunch-hour to peruse
the flamboyant carvings. Taught to fear Protestants,
you don't dare to go in, though you'd give a week's wages
to sit at the midday recitals by students from the Royal
College of Music, stand outside instead, listening –

Exsultate, jubilate, o vos animae beatae, dulcia cantica canendo.
The priory is still overlooked by the latticed towers
of Barkers, lit up so I can see two Union Jacks flapping,
but where are the red-domed buses – double-deckers –
open at the back, with landing platform and steel pole

for gripping when you jump on? Which one do you take
from your lodgings in Fulham, to get you here for 9 a.m.?
Making my way back to the station, the heels of your
new court shoes ring out on the pavement. You're here,
twenty-five, hurrying to the tube that will whisk you

to the Opera, to your narrow seat in the gods.

My Mother, Aged Fourteen

Their shoulders are hunched, as if
they are cold, or frightened, and they
are wearing shy, half-smiles, heads
cocked slightly to one side, quizzical,
wary. Their skirts are of boiled wool
and worsted, their cardigans darned,
too short in the sleeves. Their flat brogues
are laced with mud.

You are the only one wearing a jacket,
and you sit bolt upright, eyes glinting.
Is that defiance on your face, or am I
asking too much of this worn photo?
The sole of your left shoe, which you
are trying to tuck behind your right leg,
is gaping.

But Dorothy is dancing in your head,
clicking the heels of her ruby red slippers
to magic herself back to Kansas.
There's no place like home, there's no place like home.

Where will you go? To Mayes Drapery
in Fermoy, or to William Hill Bookmakers,
Picadilly Circus? To rear five children
on a new Corporation housing estate in
Cork City? Your feet have chilblains.
How could you have known that your
children or your children's children would
fly to New York to buy shoes fashioned
by men with a sense of humour and names
like Manolo, Louboutin, Jimmy Choo?

And that their confections would have
names too – *Very Privé, Toutenkaboucle* –
and plunging necklines, revealing
toe cleavage? Or that they would be
cantilevered, engineered to tip hips
and bottom up and out, for optimum
bootiliciousness? What do you think of that,
my little mother, looking, with serious
intent, toward the nun who is snapping
you on your last day of schooling?
How do you like our foot candy?

The Nuns' Wall

for Donal Noonan

At night, when I bolted up the punishing
steepness of Richmond Hill, there was
the wall, and a line of heads along the top –
nuns in the moonlight. If they weren't
ghosts, how did they get up there?
Did they drag ladders from the convent
at midnight, creaky bodies in full habit
clambering up the wobbly rungs?
I had paid my dues for robbing the grapes!
Fecky Murphy led us over the wall between
the handball alley and their greenhouse.
Big, blue grapes, huge bunches of them
I sold for a penny a throw on the street.
They had us up in court for the damage
and the shortfall in communion wine
that winter, but I got off with a warning.
The father didn't let me off though,
hauling me out of the bed at five to ride
in the side-cart with the drover to our
rented field beyond the town, from where
we would drive the cattle along the road
into the mart. And then the nuns' wall.
Were they mad, or just fond of a drop,
those beaming, gap-toothed faces?

Hail, Holy Queen

They carry her through the streets
late into the night, gentlemen of the
hermandades, on a golden throne

and she has gold in her hair and gold
in her robes and golden stars encircling
her head. She swims among

the long white tapers, shouldered
by men wearing long, white robes and
pointy hoods, with slits for the eyes and they

strew pale pink rose petals at her feet
as they weave through the cobbled lanes.
It is the night of the sacrifice, the crowds shout

*Guap*a! as she glides by, for she is the beautiful one.
On Sunday, her son, the Nazarene, will rise from
the dead, and she will be carried to the bullring

to bless the first *corrida*, through tunnelled
chambers to the small chapel where three
matadors will kiss her hand and ask her

for their lives – *Salve, Salve, Regina, llena de gracia plena!*
Which of these will brandish the bull's
ear, which sit beside the chief of police

at the victor's dinner, which will eat
the bull's testicles? Three tears
will glint on the plaster face of the statue

as young women in short skirts and high
heels take their places on the stone
benches, some close enough to smell

the sweaty *bolero*, see the pouting lips
as the young matador plunges his sword
between shoulder blades. A bull's knees will

knock, black cheeks will hit the ground, blood
pouring from a mouth into bright yellow sand.
In the chapel, tears will fall from burning candles

to stone flags. The fighter will return
to lay a rose at the feet of the statue,
beg her to turn her eyes of mercy toward him.

Virgin of the Rocks

Go on, Ann Lovett, crawl into the grotto
and join the Blessed Lady there, the one you
prayed to at the railings when your mother
held you by the hand. Water is streaming down
your school tights and the pain is making it hard
for you to move. Go on! Lie down and let your
long hair hang over the cold stones, over your belly,
let the small head come out between your legs
in the grotto cut high in the rock outside Granard,
on the last day of January, nineteen-eighty-four.

Let the small head come out and let the weight
of your heart ballast you to the grotto of your
blood, as the thick liquid starts to trickle down
your thighs, over the stones, a red waterfall
washing the Lady's alabaster feet. Whimper now,
Ann Lovett, cry to the circlet of stars, to the
corn-flower-blue eyes turned forever to the sky!
Swaddle your little scrap in Her ice-cold skirts!
Offer Her a lily, as the statue of the girl has done
all the years of your fifteen, the stone girl

in the grotto, holding the white bloom, praying
to the Holy Mother – *Oh clement, oh loving, oh
sweet virgin Mary, pray for us who have recourse to Thee!*
– lift up your blue lily, your silent boy, you prayed
to him in your belly, the secret of your small bed,
couldn't say the word you heard whispered
by your mother and your grandmother, a word
that could not be said aloud. Say it out loud now,
Ann Lovett, on this last night of January. Then
raise your heavy head from the rocks and pray.

Flux

Not only her stone face, laid back staring in the ferns,
But everything the scoop of the valley contains begins to move
– Eiléan Ní Chuilleanáin, 'Pygmalion's Image'

What is it, the one thing that moves
in this field where no one goes?
Not only her stone face, but all of her
marble body becomes milk-white
                    flesh
                              a girl

she sprints to the stream, slips in
and floats on the melt-waters tumbling
from the rocks above

Her ears fill with sounds: wriggling
of a zesty adder in the weeds
scuttling of a rabbit, its
                    bob-
                              tail

halfway back into its burrow
up-draught of wind in the feathers
of a jackdaw as it springs
from a branch

Her eyes are awash with the green
fruitiness of grass, a cloud
of whirring mayflies, a fox plunging
under a hedge with a goose
by the throat

soft
      white
            feathers
  float
      on the
           air

The veiled voices
of blades of grass blowing westward
awaken her blood, whispering

There will be secrets
vanishing acts
You will love
everything
that moves
as you do
and you will be
a bystander
as it all
disappears
down
the rabbit-
hole

She lies back in the ferns, flexing tendons
      A natterjack
          toad
             hops

from nowhere onto her broad thigh, chrysolite
glinting on the white

Valentine

The girls are in their knickers again.
It's that time of year. There are hearts –
red, plush or sparkly – dangling in windows,
and teddy bears, and girls. Undressed.
It must be cold under the white lights
of the display. The yellow street lamps add
a sickly glow to the anemic bodies. They look
pinched, the thin girls in their frillies – pale
pink lace balcony bras and high-rise briefs
with touches of white satin. One girl
stares out, brazenly, a ring-leader of sorts.
She's the one who has graduated to wearing
scarlet and black, with sheer stockings and
suspender-belt. The works.

The new storms – Gertrude, Henry –
are blowing in from America, up-scuttling
bins, rivers. There are ice crystals in the
low-flying clouds, causing rainbow effects.
A child on his way home from school stops
to take in the hearts, the teddies, the scanties,
mesmerised by their magical affinities.
I stand there imagining what happens
at 4 a.m., when there's only a dim night-light
burning, and the *tableau vivant* starts to move.
The mannequins peel red tinfoil from heart-
shaped chocolates and scoff them, then lie
under heavy blankets dragged from the next
window and hold each other. Sleep.

Nettle Paper

for Helen O'Connor

Helen is making nettle paper.
We walked the forest path with her
to gather the long stalks, growing in fat clumps
along the lake shore.

Cecilia called the names of the hedgerow-
flowers – tufted vetch, dog violet,
meadowsweet – caught sight of a newt,
skittering under clover.

The quiet of the woodland is deceptive.
On straining to listen again I heard at first
my thoughts, spinning-jennies falling through
green, and pine needles and cones crackling

beneath unseen feet and claws, then
the singing of thin branches swinging
on their hinges, pulling against bark.
Stretching my ears further, I heard base notes

of a breeze in the ash, sending whispers
across the lake, little billows,
and a very low hum from the echo-chamber
of the ancient glacial bowl.

In a book I saw an image of a nettle coat
pierced with pins, a garment of shaming.
But Helen's nettle paper is see-through, pea-green
a moiré lake's screen, or grasshoppers' wings –

a mossy cobweb from which she will make
lacy forest knickers, panties that unveil
umbels and tendrils and silken donkey ears
listening for what's kicking up its heels

under the stinging nettles' cover.

Calvary

Three trees stand on the brim
of the lake, on a slight incline,
for all the world like crosses
on the Hill of Golgotha.

The good thief and the bad thief
are in verdant health but the horse-
chestnut standing between them
is dead. Its bald form cuts

a shocking figure in mid-summer
Monaghan, where all is emerald,
lime, apple greens – bosky, ferny
mossy. The crucified tree stands

at maybe thirty feet, dwarfing
the other two, so that I want to say
a father, with a child on either side.
What happened to the old man

to stop the juices from flowing
through his venous tissue, stop
his respiratory system from
converting light to sugar? Must he

stay planted here, forever dead, in full view
of his children, while the blind universe
whirls its catherine wheels round him?
Today, for example, nifty white waves

are barreling over the surface of the lake,
but the upright corpse does not respond

to the wind's tickling, its ashen branches
poking dead fingers at an ice-cream sky.

Will no one take it down ? Would its old bones
not feed a stove, even if they no longer
move to the wind's creaky tune, no longer
bounce conkers off passing caterpillars ?

The House That Will Never Be

It may take a few years to build the house
you refuse to believe in, the house that will
never be. I see us humping stone and timber,
with the help of the locals. We will build on
rock carved in terraces rising from the sea,
beneath a canopy of carob and orange.
The walls will be powder blue, the floors
yellow sand. A stack of wood will be piled
beside the kitchen stove, and by way of a sink,
a capacious enamel bowl. In the hallway,
a bronze brazier will burn olive stones and
husks from the garden, warming us on our
return from village or shore, and a wooden
rail with pegs will hold our battered straw hats
and baskets.

I know you spit on the twin studies, one each
for you and me, with walnut tables and straight-
backed chairs, and small casement windows
framing the distant hills. When the winds blow
down through the valley, we will light our pine-
wood fires and sit and listen to the crackle.
You will write all night, I will write by day, and
sometimes your rhythm will be that of my footsteps
pacing over your head. Our hens will run giddily
among the fallen fruit, and at night, our lamp
will be seen for miles, a shepherd's fire
at the far end of a dark field. And oh,
the dreaming that will go on in that warm,
quiet house high above the world, the house
that will never be.

The Crooked Man of Chinchón

The surprise of the Plaza Mayor,
a perfect circle, cupped by latticed
balconies, with sand underfoot
and a wrought iron lamp-post
at the bull's-eye. Tiered seats
are garlanded in red and yellow
and in summer, amateur matadors

taunt young bulls in the arena.
All day I sleep, till flagstones cool
and I can take my seat at the bar
beneath the wooden boxes, wait
for the old man's traversal.
Starched and pleated, but crooked,
he leans heavily on his stick as he creaks

across the empty circus each night at nine.
He's thin as an eyelash in the dust,
thin as the minute hand on the clock
of the bell-tower, and as he moves
slowly along the diagonal, all my dead
move into formation behind him:
my thin father – bent over a stick, too –

my mother with her one breast,
eleven aunts and uncles, countless
cousins. With them troop the dead
yet to come, their names refusing
to be written in the sand. And we
are there too, you and I, in the white
bull-ring, each hot, empty evening of July

as the crooked man paddles in a pool
of dusty shadows, as the spider-leg
clock-hands hit nine, as the bell-notes
fall into the wooden bowl of the plaza.
It's not hard to imagine black horses
in procession, festooned with pompoms,
and women in black lace mantillas,
hiding their faces behind fans.

Transportation in a Watery World

And I'll put you in the dug-out canoe,
like Moses in his basket of reeds,
sent down-river, out of harm's way.
I'll take you in that Seminole barque
and we'll travel the waterways of Florida –
the St John's River, and the glades –
gliding on the tracery of green veins
through swamps and grassy marshlands.
The grey beards of low-hanging oaks will
tickle your wrists as you loll in the prow,
and I'll row for all I'm worth. No Indian
will shoot poison-dipped arrows at us
from the mangroves, and there will be no
white-water rapids. The glades will cocoon us
in a lace shawl of light as we slip along, drift
and sometimes rock gently in our floating
cradle. The canoe will move slowly, but
endlessly, through the watery green.

NOTES

pp. 15–17. 'Flânerie of the Beaver'
The poem takes its origin in a 'literary walk' I took in the Quartier
Latin area of Paris in 2016. The walk was conducted by the Belgian
poet, Eugène Savitzkaya, and the poem records Savitzkaya's
words and actions in the course of the walk. The poem ends with
my version of 2 lines taken from a street plaque on rue Rollin,
highlighted by Savitzkaya, in memory of the Romanian-French
poet Benjamin Fondane. Fondane was taken from rue Rollin by
the Nazis in 1944, and he died later that year in Auschwitz. The
inscription on the plaque, taken from Fondane's poem 'L'Exode',
reads as follows:

'souvenez-vous seulement que j'étais innocent
et que, tout comme vous, mortels de ce jour-là,
j'avais eu, moi aussi, un visage marqué
par la colère, par la pitié et la joie,
un visage d'homme, tout simplement!'